ENRICHED DOG

Many of our activities include videos to illustrate the instructions. Whenever an exercise has this **symbol** ▶ you'll be able to watch a matching video.

Scan this code to find the corresponding clip!

Go to **www.enricheddog.com/pages/videos** to find the corresponding clip!

FLEECE ROLL-UPS

Cut fleece (or any material) into strips of 8-12" long by 1 ½-2" wide. Take 10-20 fleece strips, put a few pieces of kibble/treats at one end and roll them up. Fleece, treat, roll, fleece, treat and roll, you get it!

For added fun you can:
- Put the fleece roll-ups in a Tupperware or box.
- Hide each roll-up around the house for a treasure hunt game.
- Use a few pot lids to hide the rolls and have your dog guess which lid the roll-ups are under.

30 - 60 min.
first time
5 - 10 min.
after that

Under $20

ENRICHED DOG

SNIFFARI

Imagine the pure joy your dog feels using their nose and natural instincts to sniff and follow a scent. This is like winning the lottery for a dog!

How to get ready for your Sniffari:
- Bring a training lead (10'/20'/30' leash) and let your dog explore (safely of course).
- Let your dog sniff that fire hydrant for 10 minutes!
- New places are super-duper fun for dogs!

20 - 90 min.

FREE!

Don't think of the distance. Instead, pick how much TIME you have and let your dog's nose take YOU for a walk! Where will they take you??

SNUFFLE BOX

Grab an empty box and go for a walk in the woods or around your yard and collect a bunch of sticks, leaves and whatever else you want to add to your Snuffle Box.

- Throw some kibble or treats in the box and let your dog sniff and forage for the goodies.

- Instead of food, you can just let them sniff all the different items you brought in from outside.

- You can hide a toy(s) amongst the leaves and branches.

- Ask some friends with cats and dogs to save some fur and add that to the box!

10 - 15 min. to make

FREE!

5

ENRICHED DOG

DOUBLE DOUBLE ▶

Next time you go through the drive-through keep the to-go tray for some mental enrichment fun!

- Put kibble in each section and put another tray on top of it.

- Your dog will need to figure out how to get the top one off to get to the goods.

- Put kibble on the ground and put the trays over each pile of kibble.

- Tie a string through a few trays and suspend it. Put kibble in each section.

Under 5 min.

FREE!

*If you're not from 🇨🇦 'Double Double' is a way to ask for a coffee with two creams and two sugars.' "Hi there! I'd like a double double and a honey dip donut eh!"

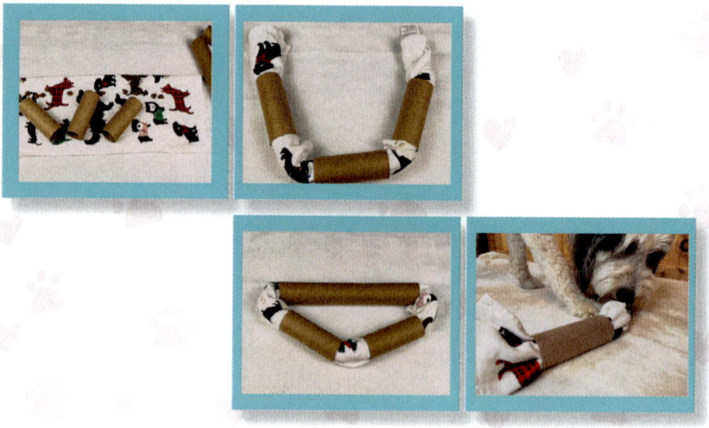

ENRICHED DOG

SAUSAGE ROLL ▶

Start saving all of your toilet and paper towel rolls! There are MANY mental games you can play with the tubes.

To prepare the Sausage Roll:
- Take a tea towel and lay it flat on the table.
- Sprinkle some treats all over the towel.
- Roll the towel tightly.
- Stuff it through the toilet paper roll.
- Add a few more rolls to make it like a sausage!

10 - 15 min.

Under $5

Your pooch has to figure out how to remove the toilet paper roll around the towel to get what's inside.
- Will they grab it and shake?
- Try to tear off the rolls?
- Paw at it?

Place your bets and see who wins!

PASS ME THE WINE!

Next time you go buy some wine or cold ones, be sure to grab a wine box or a case of beer for some fun enrichment.

- Put your dog's breakfast or dinner in the box and voilà!

For added difficulty:
- Stuff some tea towels or toys in the box. Your dog will need to remove them first before getting to the goodies.

Under 5 min.

FREE!

Easy breezy

SCATTERFEED ▶

Take the kibble outside for a fun sniffing adventure! It's like an Easter Egg Hunt for your dog.

- Lazy Version - Throw a handful of kibble in backyard. Yup. It's that Easy.

- Non-Lazy Version - Strategically place kibble around your yard. Hide the kibble in higher places so your dog learns to sniff up and down.

Under 5 min.

FREE!

ENRICHED DOG

BiLLY JEANS

Look in your closet and find some old jeans.
- Hide treats/kibble in the pockets.
- Sprinkle some on the legs and roll it up!!

Under 5 min.

FREE!

Easy **breezy**

SEARCH & RESCUE

Take your dog's favourite toy and play with it. Get your dog engaged in the toy.

- Ask for a sit or stay, or have someone hold your dog while you go and hide it.
- Give your dog the release cue "Go find it!" and watch your dog sniff and figure out where their toy is.
- Once they find it, say YESSS! And let them play with their toy for 30-60 seconds.
- Then trade for a treat and repeat.

Have **fun!**

Play as many reps as you want! Have fun!

FREE!

ENRICHED DOG

Do You Know the Muffin Man?

Here's a super simple game!
- Grab your burnt out muffin tins that you never use.
- Put kibble in the muffin holes.
- Put any kind of ball or toys over each hole.

Your dog has to figure out how to get to the food by removing the objects on top.
- You can flip the tin upside down for another fun game.
- Wrap it in a towel or blanket.
- Put it in a box.

Easy breezy

Under 5 min.

FREE!

(If you have one. Under $5 if you don't)

ENRICHED DOG

LOST & FOUND

Want to get lost on purpose? Your dog will enjoy this activity as it's their NOSE that will be playing the game.

- Find a wooded area with a good trail system.
- Set your timer...30, 40, 90 minutes.
- Bring a GPS and let your dog take YOU on an adventure!
- Left, right, this way, that way…let your dog's natural instincts kick in and lead the way!
- When the timer rings, it's time for you to find your way back!

Get the kids involved and now it's THEIR turn to lead everyone out.

30 - 90 min. adventures!

FREE!

SCENT TRAIL - BACON STRIPS

This one is easy and your dog will LOVE it!

- Take one or two pieces of uncooked bacon and tie a long piece of string at one end.
- Go outside and drag the bacon all around on the ground
making a yummy scent trail.
- Every so often place a piece of treat/kibble along the scent trail.
- At the end of the trail leave a bunch of treats/kibble…JACKPOT!

10 - 15 min.

Under $5

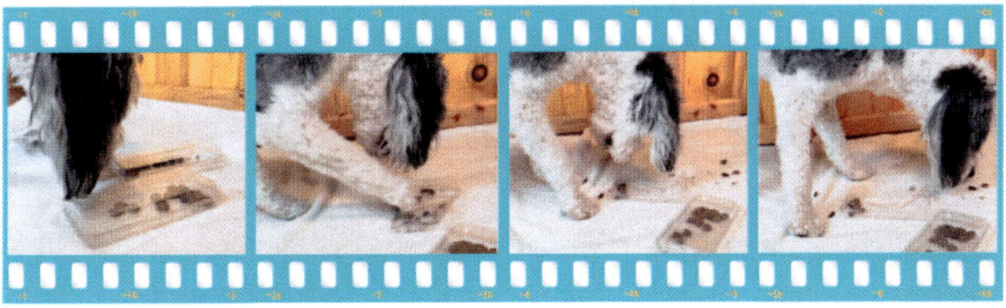

ENRICHED DOG

HERBALICIOUS ▶

What to do with all those clam-like containers that fresh herbs come in? You can use them for a fun mental enrichment game for your pooch!

- Fill them up with kibble/treats and have your dog try to open them up.
- Fill them with some wet or raw food.
- Hide them around the house for a fun game of hide a treat.

If your dog is struggling with an enrichment game, make it easy for them at the start.

Under 5 min.

FREE!

Recycle bin fun!

We want enrichment to be FUN!

ENRICHED DOG

PASS ME THE OJ! ▶

Take an empty bottle of orange juice, cut a few holes and fill it with your dog's breakfast or dinner.
If you are worried about the cap being eaten (I'm looking at you Labradors and Doodles!) you can throw it out and use that hole for the food to come out of.

- Put some fleece strips in the holes so your dog has to pull out the strips for the food to come out.

For added difficulty
- Hide the bottle(s) around the house.
- Wrap the bottles in a towel.
- Take a clothes hamper and fill it with old blankets and sheets and bury the bottles in there for some digging fun!

Under 10 min.

FREE!

ENRICHED DOG

BROWN BAG ▶

Next time you grab your groceries, ask for some paper grocery bags, or order some take-out and keep your greasy bags!

Throw some kibble in each bag and have your dog tear the bag open for some added fun!

Under 5 min.

FREE!

Easy breezy

14

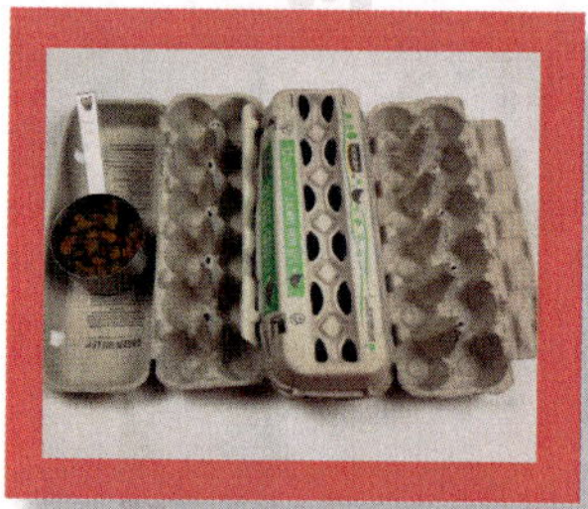

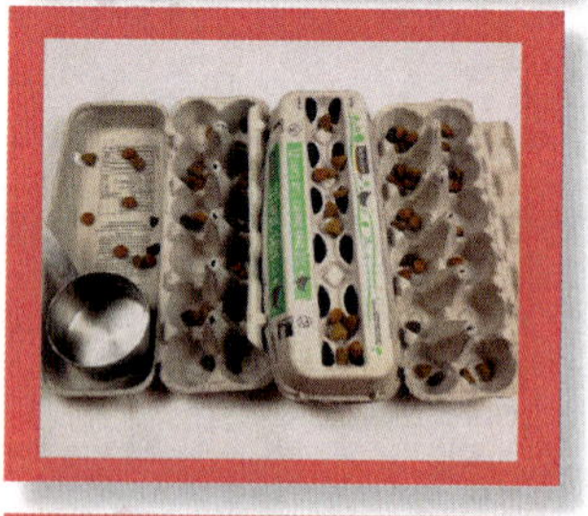

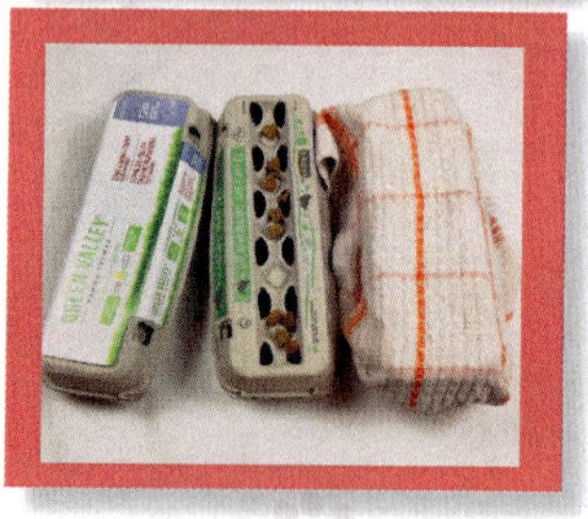

ENRICHED DOG

EGG-CELENT! ▶

Save your egg cartons for a variety of mental fun! Your dog will need to figure out how to get the food out of the carton.
To make it easy at first, you can leave it a little open and then close it when they get the hang of it!

- Put some kibble inside the carton and close the lid.
- Wrap it up in a towel (put kibble in the towel too!)
- Flip it upside down and add kibble in the nooks & crannies.

Under 5 min.

FREE!

Easy breezy

15

Digging Pit (inside)

There are certain breeds that just LOOOVE to dig because that's what they were bred for! Instead of trying to teach a dog NOT to dig, let's give them a safe and appropriate outlet for it.

A fun Digging Pit inside your house can be:

- **Smaller dogs:** Take a clothes hamper and put towels and old sheets inside. Hide some yummy treats or kibble and a few favourite toys within the hamper and let your dog dig around looking for the goodies!

- **Larger dogs:** Grab some old comforters, sheets or sleeping bags and pick a corner in your house and make a big mountain of blankets.

5 - 10 min. to setup

FREE!

Let's Go Shopping!

For your dog's birthday or a special occasion, bring your pooch to the local pet store and let them choose a bone or toy.

You can also visit a pet friendly store like:

- Hardware stores
- Outdoor garden centres
- Farmers' markets
- Local Humane Society

10 min.
Depends how far you have to drive.

FREE!

Minus gas money and anything you buy

A new environment is VERY mentally stimulating for a dog. All those new smells, sights and sounds! When you get home, they will sleep the night away!

ENRICHED DOG

PASS ME A TOWEL! ▶

Take any kind of towel and:

- Lay it down flat, placing kibble in a row at one end of the towel before rolling it a few times. Place another row of kibble, roll it up a few more times, and so on.
- You can fold the towel in different ways as well.

Under 5 min.

FREE!

For added difficulty: Add a knot or two in the towel.

17

ENRICHED DOG

RUSSIAN DOLLS ▶

Does your dog like to shred paper or boxes? If you answered YES, this will be such a fun mental game for your pup!

Look in your recycling bin and take out any cardboard boxes.

- Cracker boxes
- Tea boxes
- Delivery boxes
- Pizza box!!!

Once you have 3-5 boxes from smallest to largest you will:

- Take your smallest box and put some delicious treats or kibble in it.
- Take a slightly bigger box and put the small one in the bigger one and sprinkle some treats/kibble inside.
- Put those two boxes in a larger box.
- Repeat again and again!

5 - 10 min.

FREE!

Now your dog has not only 1 box to open, but THREE, FOUR or even FIVE boxes! Your dog will be snoozing in no time because that was a LOT of mental power!

ENRICHED DOG

ICE ICE BABY ▶

This is a fun enrichment game when it is hot outside.

Items you will need:
- Stainless steel bowl
- Small toys
- Yummy treats/kibble
- Chew/bone

Instructions:
- Fill up the stainless steel bowl with 2" of water. Put a few treats and a toy in the water and put the bowl in the freezer.
- Once frozen, add another layer of goodies and water and freeze again.
- Add a final layer of water and treats. This time add a bone or large toy. Make sure it is something that will stick halfway out of the water and freeze again.
- Bring the bowl outside for your pup to lick and enjoy their pupsicle!

Few hours for final results.

Under $5

BAG-O-TOYS

What dog doesn't like a stuffed toy?! Some may tear it open, but a lot of dogs won't destroy their prized toy. I STILL have some of my previous dog's (Breeze) stuffies from 15+ years ago!

- Go to local thrift shops and get bags of stuffies for cheap.
- Freecycle sites! I have picked up four garbage bags of stuffies over the years. I keep a bag in my car and whenever I visit my 'godson' Ozzy, the Great Pyrenees, he gets a new stuffie from Auntie.
- Ask! Post on social media asking for any old stuffies or dog toys.
- Too many stuffies? Donate them to a shelter or rescue!

You don't have to spend a lot of money on ways to tire out your monster puppy or crazy doodle!!

Depends how much effort you put into it

FREE!

Or whatever you are willing to spend

BALLOON FUN!

Happy Birthday to you! Happy Birthday to you!
Some dogs love to bounce a balloon off their snout! Toss the balloon to them, they will jump up and BOOP the balloon back to you!

Under 5 min.

Under $5

Once your pooch gets the hang of it, you can:
- Get a small basketball net and teach your dog to shoot some hoops.
- Count to see how many times you can keep the balloon in the air!
- Get two people and teach your dog to hit the balloon to both of you.

Tip! Put a sock over the balloon for added safety.

ENRICHED DOG

BOX SHREDDER ▶

Some dogs really enjoy shredding and ripping apart boxes or paper. As long as they are not ingesting the cardboard or paper let them at it!

Other fun stuff to shred:

- Old phone books
- Kids homework
- Bills
- Love letters from an ex

Under 5 min.

FREE!

HULA HOOP

Bring back the '80s minus the spandex and teased hair!

Grab a hula hoop or two and have your dog:
- Jump through the hoop.
- Hang a sheet on one side and make it like a shoot that your dog has to go through.
- Put the hula hoop on the ground and send your dog to the center of the hoop. Add some obedience training like sit, down, puppy push-ups, touch etc. inside the hoop.

Under 5 min.

$5 - $10

21

ENRICHED DOG

What the floof?

You walk into a room and all over the floor is white fluffy stuffing from your dog's beloved plush toy! Sigh! Another toy destroyed...but wait!!!

A lot of dogs like to "kill" their stuffies. It is instinctual and absolutely SATISFYING for some dogs to grab, shake, dissect...and then sit there with this silly grin of satisfaction.

If your dog likes to take the stuffing out of their toys, let them.... (as long as they don't eat the stuffing or squeakers!) Put the floof back into the dismembered limbs and let them at it again...and again...and again!

- You can even put treats/kibble in the toy for added fun.

Under 5 min.

FREE!

ENRICHED DOG

LICKITY SPLIT ▶

Licky mats are a great tool to keep your dog busy while you work on body desensitization exercises like cutting nails, grooming, teeth brushing, cleaning ears etc.

Smear your dog's favourite food on the licky mat like:

- Plain yogurt
- Natural peanut butter (NO xylitol - toxic for dogs)
- Wet dog food
- Pumpkin
- Mother-in-law's meatloaf

Under 5min

Under $10

You can use:

- Silicone pot holder
- Muffin tins
- Wall of the shower/tub (great for bathtime!)
- Your forehead

23

PAPER ROLL-UPS ▶

Have you ever received a box in the mail that had a bunch of paper used to pack the item you purchased? There are a lot of fun mental games you can play with these like:

- Lay the paper flat and sprinkle kibble/treats on top before rolling it back up, like you would a carpet.
- Put kibble/treats in the middle and scrunch it up.
- Fold the paper and stack it like newspaper, putting kibble in between the folds.

5 - 10 min.
depending which activity you do.

FREE!

ENRICHED DOG

POCKETS FULL OF FUN! ▶

That shoe organizer you have hanging in your closet with all those fancy shoes you SWEAR you are going to wear but, in reality, it's been since 2005 that you've actually worn them?

Turn your shoe organizer into a fun sniffing game for your pup:

- Lay it on the floor and hide kibble in the pouches.
- Hang it from a chair or counter for a different scent game, making the dog sniff up and down.
- Stuff toys in the pouch so your dog has to take the toy out first to get to the kibble.

5 -10 min.

FREE!

(If you have one. $10-$20 if you don't)

25

ENRICHED DOG

STiNKY SHOES! ▶

Line-up your shoes/boots/heels/slippers in a row and hide treats in between them. Let your dog sniff around, inhale all those lovely smells and find the treats.

Easy breezy

5 min.

FREE!

JUG-A-LUG

Instead of returning your empty blue jug of water, you can use it for a variety of enrichment fun! Take a drill and make some holes in it big enough for kibble/treats to fall out of. Or you can throw the jug in the backyard for the dogs that love to push around and herd objects.

Under 5 min.
Once holes are made.

Minus deposit fee!

ENRICHED DOG

UPRIGHT TP ▶

Remember earlier when I said to save up your toilet paper and paper towel rolls? Here's another idea: Grab a container or two…or THREE! Stand the rolls upright within the container and sprinkle the kibble/treats in each tube. Your dog has to figure out how to move the tubes to get to the food.

5 min. to set up!

FREE!

What will your dog do?

- Grab each one delicately?
- Paw the container?
- Grab it and SHAKE it?

27

ENRICHED DOG

HiDE & SEEK

Think back as a child playing hide & seek with the neighbourhood kids! So fun!
You can start this game simply by hiding behind a chair or sofa.
- One person holds onto the dog and the other person goes and hides.
- If your dog is having a hard time finding you, blow your breath.
- Yes, you read that right. Your breath stinks! Well, it has a lot of scent molecules that your dog will pick up on because...

Under 5 min.

FREE!

DOG'S HAVE 300 MILLION SCENT RECEPTORS! We only have 7 million. They will smell your stinky breath and find you!

Easy breezy

BUBBLES!

This is a fun game for our two and four-legged kids!

One easy recipe for homemade bubbles is:
- 1/4 cup of liquid dish soap
- 1/2 cup of water
- 1 tsp sugar
- 1 bouillon cube.

Under 15 min.

Under $10

Place a bouillon cube in 1/2 cup of water and then 30 seconds in the microwave until it is dissolved. Mix all ingredients in a small bowl and stir gently.
Grab your favourite bubble wand and have a friendly competition between the kids and dog to see who can pop the most bubbles!

ENRICHED DOG

KONG CLASSIC. Timeless. ORiginal. ▶

The classic red Kong is a staple for your dog's enrichment basket. This versatile enrichment toy can be used in many different ways:
- Stuff it with kibble, wet food and freeze it (see bonus recipes on page 42).
- Tie it to the back of the crate to make the crate a fun space.
- Stuff your Kongs and hide a bunch around the house for your dog to sniff out!

5-10 minutes to stuff + freezing time.

$15-$40

various sizes

29

ENRICHED DOG

HATS & TUQUES ▶

Grab all your baseball hats and winter tuques and use them for a fun game of Hide-A-Treat!

- Spread the hats and tuques around on the floor, grab some kibble/treats and hide underneath or inside the hats.

- Put them in a row and hide only 1 kibble/treat and have your dog find it.

- You can teach them to sit when they find the treat and reward from your hand (don't let them eat the hidden treat).

- Instead of food, you can hide your dog's favourite toy for them to sniff out.

5 - 10 min. setup

FREE!

ENRICHED DOG

Snuffle Mats ▶

Sniff sniff sniff!!! Your dog will enjoy using their instincts to sniff and forage for food using the snuffle mats. You can purchase one or make your own.

Here's how to make one:
- Cut LOTS...and I mean LOTS of strips of fleece 6"-8" long x 2" wide.
- Get a sink mat or rubber mat with holes.
- Take a strip and weave it through a hole and tie it once. Repeat.
- An hour later, you've done two rows! Whew hew!!!

LOTS!
4 hrs Easy!
5 min. once made or purchased.

Under $15

DYI ($20-$40 if you buy new)

ENRICHED DOG

TOY BASKET ▶

This is an easy one! Grab a handful of kibble/treats and throw it in your dog's toy basket.

Easy breezy

Under 5 min.

FREE!

INDOOR AGILITY ▶

Too hot outside? Too cold? This is a fun mental and physical enrichment game to play with your dog. You can set up your own agility course inside your house! You can use a variety of items around your home like:

- Broom handles for the pup to go over or under
- Blankets for makeshift tunnels
- Chairs
- Your couch etc.

10 - 20 min.
To set-up.

FREE!

Do this for 10- 15 minutes and your dog will be snoring on the couch in no time!

ENRICHED DOG

MONTHLY SUBSCRIPTION BOX ▶

There are some PAWESOME subscription boxes available. Imagine your dog's excitement every month when they get to open a box of goodies JUST FOR THEM!

Generally these boxes have:
- Plush toy
- Chew toy or food dispensing toy
- Various treats
- A bone

There are lots of companies to choose from depending on what country you are in. Visit https://go.referral-candy.com/share/DDWKSXL or $20 off your first Woof Pack subscription box.

Only waiting the days in between boxes!

Monthly subscription vary from $30-$50/month

33

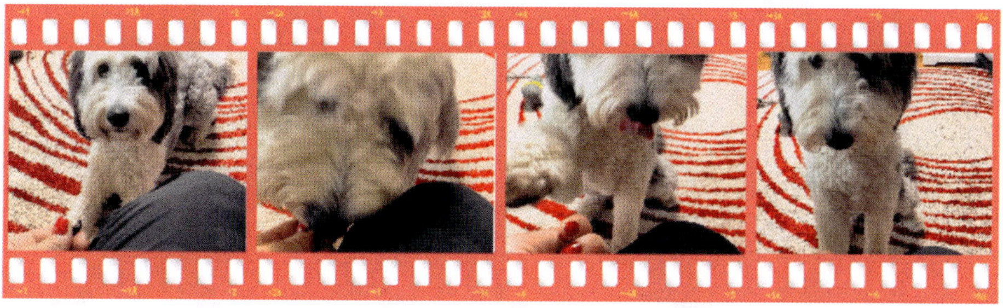

TAKE-iT / LEAVE-iT

This is a fun training game to help with impulse control.

- Hold a treat in your fingers, next to your knee and tell your dog "Take-it!"
- Take another treat and put it in the palm of your hand and make a fist.
- Hold your fist next to your knee and say "Leave-it!" Your dog may sniff, paw or nibble on your hand. Just keep it still, don't move and don't say anything. Your dog may try to paw at it and nibble at your fingers. Tip: Tuck in your thumb!
- The MOMENT your dog backs away from your hand, say YESSS! and reward.
- Using different values of treats like chicken or cheese will be much harder for your dog to leave-it vs kibble or a milk bone.
- Start with lower level treats and work your way up to the yummy stuff.

Train for 5-10 repetitions.

FREE!

ENRICHED DOG

CUPS ▶

Classic game of putting something under one of three cups and moving them around. Then your dog has to guess which cup it's under.

You can use:
- Red beer pong cups
- Tupperware
- Pot lids
- Empty soap or toothpaste boxes

Under 5 min.

FREE!

Grab your cups and put a treat under one of them and move the three cups however you like - around each other, to the left, to the right, circle, circle, circle, switcheroo fake-out....and VOILÀ! Have your pooch guess which one the treat is under, and once they get it -- Yesss! and reward.

35

TUG-O-LOT

This is a fun dog toy for children to make! It will keep them busy for a while and then you can have a good game of tug with your pooch!!!

- You need four long strips of material. You can use t-shirts, jeans, fleece etc.
- To get the long tug toy, like in the video, you will need 4 strips that are cut 65 inches long by 1 ½-2" inches wide.
- Tie the end and then make your square knot (instructions in the video).
- Easy version is taking three strips and braiding them.

Tug is a great mental and physical exercise and you can use it as a training opportunity for leave-it or let go homework. Your dog will be so tired after a round of tug!

20-30 minutes to make the square knot tug.
10 minutes to make a braid.

FREE!

if you use fabric around the house. Under $10 to buy new.

ENRICHED DOG

CONE HEAD

If you have a dog that takes fetch to the next level, try getting them to use their nose for half the game, if not more. Instead of adrenaline, adrenaline, adrenaline, ball, ball, ball, you hide their ball under a small orange cone and your dog has to sniff it out. They are now using their nose which helps reduce heart rate, calms them and it's all brain power!

5 - 10 min.
To setup

FREE!

with items around your house.
$5 - $10 at discount stores.

If you don't have cones, you can use:
- Plastic cups.
- Tupperware containers
- Pot lids.
- Empty yogurt containers.

37

ENRICHED DOG

ADVENT CALENDAR ▶

Here's how your dog can enjoy a variety of advent calendars:

- Regular Advent Calendars: After eating all those chocolates, clean the calendar well before you hide some kibble for your dog to tear into.

- Reusable Advent Calendars: These are really great as you have multiple boxes to use. Put some kibble in one of the boxes and let your dog find it!

- TIP! Use only the same box(es) to put food in. Mark these with a sticker or with an X.

- Hanging/handmade calendar - The two reusable calendars featured in the video were gifted on a Freecycle site - perfect to hide kibble in!

Under 5 min.

FREE!
If your kids have any.

ENRICHED DOG

ACTIVITY MAT ▶

If you sew or know someone who is good with a sewing machine, have them make you a custom mat! Or you can also purchase them in stores and online.

The Activity Mat can include:
- Folds
- Flaps
- Roll-ups
- Pockets
- Dragons & unicorns

Be creative! What do you think your dog would like best?

Under 5 minutes to get ready with food.

$20 - $40 for DIY

depending on cost of materials. $40-$60 custom made.

PUZZLE TOYS ▶

There are a lot of puzzle games for dogs out there. When introducing these puzzles to your dog, keep it simple at first. It's not fun for your dog if it's too frustrating. To increase the difficulty you can:

- Add peanut butter so that it is harder to remove movable objects.
- Wrap it in a blanket/towel.
- Put it in a box.
- Hide it under some dirty clothes in a hamper.

Under 5 min.

$20-$50

depending on the puzzle toy.

ENRICHED DOG

WHACK-A-MOLE ▶

You may have seen this one on social media! To play this game:

- Take a cardboard box and cut 6-12 holes, 1-2" wide, on one side.

- Cut open the back part of the box so that you can put your hand inside and underneath the holes.

- Then grab a hotdog, carrot or toy and quickly push it up through one of the holes and see what your dog does.

- If they try to grab it, quickly pull it back into the box and go to another hole and do the same thing over and over again. Make sure to reward your dog every now and then to avoid frustration.

10-15 minutes to make it the first time.

FREE!

$5 for a pack of wieners

LEAF BLOWER

Depending where you are in the world, fall is a beautiful time of year and is a great opportunity for some fun for your dog and children! Grab your rake or leaf blower and make a HUGE pile of leaves, have some fun and create some memories!!

- Throw a ball or stick in the middle of the pile for your dog to go jump in and find it.
- Hide the kids in the pile and have your dog sniff them out.
- Need 15-20 minutes of peace and quiet? Throw your dog's dinner in the pile and you will have time to bbq and enjoy a cold bevy!

20-60 min. depending on how many trees you have!

FREE!

JOLLY BALL

Do you have a dog that loves to herd or is ball obsessed? The Jolly Balls are a durable ball that was originally made for horse enrichment. There are different styles of the Jolly Ball.

- Some have a handle on them, for dogs that like to chase but also carry the ball.
- Others are made from a harder plastic, these are great for dogs that like to push and herd the ball around.
- Some balls are made from a tough rubber so dogs can still get their teeth into it but not puncture it.

Check out Treibball. It's a wonderful sport for dogs that enjoy this form of enrichment.

5-15 minute game will help tire out your pooch!

Under $50

depending which ball you get.

Bonus!

With the purchase of this book you have access to download a free Two-Week Enrichment Schedule and Kong Recipes! Scan this code to get yours!

Visit this link to get yours!
www.enricheddog.com/pages/freebies

About the Author:

Kyla Denault is the founder, owner and head trainer of **Easy Breezy Dog Training.** She grew up in Northern Ontario and moved to the Ottawa area in the late '90's and has made Orleans her home for the past 12+ years.

Across her career, Kyla has gathered a wealth of experience working with dogs and people while also staying involved in her community.

- Kyla opened up one of the first Cage-Free Dog Kennels in the early 2000s, which she ran as a successful business until selling it in 2009.

- She is a Certified Dog Trainer and earned her Dog Trainer Certification with the Ottawa Canine School in 2017. Kyla is also working towards obtaining her Certified Professional Dog Trainer Knowledge Assessed (CPDT-KA) Designation through The Certification Council for Professional Dog Trainers© (CCPDT©), the leading independent certifying organization for the dog training profession.

- Kyla currently volunteers at the Ottawa Humane Society as a Canine Behaviour Interventionist where she helps train dogs and puppies that are up for adoption.

A number of years ago, Kyla asked herself what brings her joy. Her answers were **helping people, animals and creativity.**

A Note from Kyla
I'm doing what brings me joy every single day and I absolutely love being a dog trainer, especially when I get to work with kids and puppies!

Mental enrichment is one of the first things I talk about to my clients. Engaging your dog's brain will help tire them out and will help keep you sane! All these ideas have been tested with my own pack and they love it. Hope your pooch enjoys it as well!
~Kyla.

CREDITS

Priya Aubie, copy editor
Ashlee Prestidge, copy editor
Kai Harada, video editor
Ana Steinberg Designs, graphics and ebook design

INDEX

Free exercises

Activity Mat	39
Advent Calendar	38
Bag-o-Toys	20
Balloon Fun	20
Billy Jeans	9
Box Shredder	21
Brown Bag	14
Bubbles	28
Cone Head	37
Cups	35
Digging Pit (Inside)	16
Do You Know the Muffin Man?	10
Double Double	6
Egg-celent	15
Fleece Roll-Ups	4
Hats & Tuques	30
Herbalicious	12
Hide & Seek	28
Hula Hoop	21
Ice Ice Baby	19
Indoor Agility	32
Jolly Ball	42
Jug-A-Lug	26
Kong classic. Timeless. Original.	29
Leaf Blower	42
Let's Go Shopping!	16
Lickity Split	23
Lost Found	11
Monthly Subscription Box	33
Paper Rolls Ups	24
Pass me a Towel!	17
Pass me the OJ!	13
Pass me the wine!	8
Pocket Full O Fun	25
Puzzle Toys	40
Russian Dolls	18
Sausage Roll	7
Scatterfeed	8
Scent Trail - Bacon Strips	11
Search & Rescue	9
Sniffari	5
Snuffle Box	5
Snuffle Mats	31
Stinky Shoes	26
Take-It / Leave-It	34
Toy Basket	32
Tug-o-Lot	36
Upright TP	27
Whack-A-Mole	41
What the Floof	22

S0-EVW-418